SICKNESS,
AND SCRIPTURE

SICKNESS, SUFFERING, AND SCRIPTURE

David Leyshon

THE BANNER OF TRUTH TRUST

THE BANNER OF TRUTH TRUST

3 Murrayfield Road, Edinburgh EH12 6EL, UK
P.O. Box 621, Carlisle, PA 17013, USA

ISBN-13: 978 0 85151 971 5

Typeset in 11/15 pt Sabon at
the Banner of Truth Trust
Printed in the U.S.A. by
Versa Press, Inc.,
East Peoria, IL

CONTENTS

INTRODUCTION

*I*t would be true to say that, until fairly recently in the history of the Western world, the great majority of men and women saw and accepted sickness and suffering as an inevitable feature of life in this world. High levels of infant mortality, limited medical knowledge, and the ravages of what nowadays are curable diseases, all contributed to making suffering and death an ever-present reality. Recent generations, however, think so very differently.

In the first place a scientific revolution has occurred which has become for many an object of 'faith'. This is why doctors are now blamed and even sued if a patient succumbs to illness. Sensational news reports feed the public's optimism with details of further medical breakthroughs. The impression given is that we can expect to enjoy longer lives which will be increasingly free from disease.

Equally significant has been the 'theological' shift that has also taken place in the minds of many. Man and his happiness have replaced God and his glory as the *raison d'être* of the universe. In this new view of things, men not only have the capacity to rid themselves of sickness and suffering – they have the right to good health and a happy life!

For the Bible-believing Christian, such shifts in the popular outlook might be written off as symptoms of a godless modernity. However, the entrance into some parts of the evangelical world of those who put forward a Christianized version of the above, manipulating biblical texts in the process, has brought this whole issue of our attitude to sickness and suffering much closer to home. There is now real confusion among the people of God which is seen in the many and varied answers to these important questions:

What are we to make of sickness and suffering?

And how are we to respond to them?

The aim of the following brief studies is simply to remind the Christian believer about the great foundational truths of the Word of God as they apply to this integral part of their life in this world.

Introduction

While allowing for the element of mystery that is so central to any consideration of God's providential government of the universe (human life included), these studies will investigate those aspects of the truth which God has been pleased to make known to us. Along with a clearer understanding of suffering will come a more realistic perspective on its place in the life of the believer, coupled with an eager and healthy anticipation of its ultimate banishment when the glory of the new creation is revealed at the return of our Lord and Saviour, Jesus Christ.

I

THE INEVITABILITY
OF SUFFERING

Light is sweet, and it is pleasant for the eyes to see the sun. [8] So if a person lives many years, let him rejoice in them all; but let him remember that the days of darkness will be many. All that comes is vanity. [9] Rejoice, O young man, in your youth, and let your heart cheer you in the days of your youth. Walk in the ways of your heart and the sight of your eyes. But know that for all these things God will bring you into judgment. [10] Remove vexation from your heart, and put away pain from your body, for youth and the dawn of life are vanity. [12:1] Remember also your Creator in the days of your youth, before the evil days come and the years draw near of which you will say, 'I have no pleasure in them'; [2] *before the sun and the light and the moon and the stars are darkened and the clouds return after the rain,* [3] *in the day when the keepers of the house tremble, and the strong men are bent, and the grinders cease because they are few, and those who look through the windows are dimmed,* [4] *and the doors on the street are shut – when the sound of the grinding is low, and one rises up at the sound of a bird, and all the daughters of song are brought low –* [5] *they are afraid also of what is high, and terrors are in the way; the almond tree blossoms, the grasshopper drags itself along, and desire fails, because man is going to his eternal home, and the mourners go about the streets –* [6] *before the silver cord is snapped, or the golden bowl is broken, or the pitcher is shattered at the fountain, or the wheel broken at the cistern,* [7] *and the dust returns to the earth as it was, and the spirit returns to God who gave it.* [8] *Vanity of vanities, says the Preacher; all is vanity (Eccles. 11:7–12:8).*

All we have to do is to live long enough,
and we will suffer.

D. A. Carson

2

OUTLINE

*A*dvances in medical technology in recent generations have been astonishing and far-reaching. Diseases, which once killed millions, are now effectively treated by a simple course of tablets, or even prevented altogether by vaccination. The pace of medicine's progress is unrelenting; it holds out the promise of future success in curing many of the conditions that still plague the human race. For all these blessings we should be deeply grateful to God, who in his grace has provided men with the wisdom and the materials to accomplish such wonderful things.

But this progress should not blind us to continuing realities. Optimism in some quarters that sees no limits to medical science and entertains the hope that it will bring us to the eventual conquest of death itself, is not just premature – it is tragically misplaced. For the infallible Word of God declares that 'man is destined to die', and that death will not be removed from our experience in this world until God himself intervenes at the close of human history to introduce a wholly new order of things under the headship of the Lord Jesus Christ.

Meanwhile, it is sobering to call to mind that in spite of all modern advances in the field of medical science, the life expectancy of twenty-first century man, even in the western world, remains fairly bound by the limits revealed to Moses over three thousand years ago! – 'The years of our life are seventy, or even by reason of strength eighty' (*Psa.* 90:10).

Now this unavoidable fact of death is accompanied and preceded by the process of dying. Everything and everyone in this world is growing old; and if some are spared the ravages of serious illness and accident in the prime of life (for this is a dangerous and unpredictable world), then the onset of old age will invariably bring some sort of suffering in its wake as the precursor of death. Eliphaz, one of Job's 'comforters', though at fault for the wrong application of his sound arguments to innocent and godly Job, nevertheless expressed a basic and fundamental truth when he observed that 'man is born to trouble as the sparks fly upwards.' It is a conclusion that Job himself arrives at later in the book – 'Man who is born of a woman is few of days and full of trouble'(*Job* 14:1).

But perhaps the most graphic of all the biblical presentations of the sober, universal reality of suffering as crystallized in old age, is found in the closing chapter of Ecclesiastes. Here, against this dark back-cloth, is urged upon the young the absolute necessity of the fear of the Lord.

NOTE

Ecclesiastes 12:2-7: It is probable that the language used in these verses is a poetic way of outlining the decline in our physical and mental powers that accompanies the aging process.

QUESTIONS

1. Does this highly descriptive passage see old age and its accompanying difficulties as a possibility, probability, or certainty? What conclusion does the writer draw in verse 8, when viewing human life as detached from its eternal, God-centred perspective?

2. What does the writer call his readers to in Ecclesiastes 11:8-10 and 12:1 in the light of the inevitability of old age, suffering, and death? Why is this more important than medical insurance, making a will, and financial planning?

3. If you are someone who has not yet suffered to a significant degree, have you faced up to the inevitability of future suffering? If you have suffered or are suffering, what should you be urging on those who have not?

2

THE SOURCE
OF SUFFERING

*The Lord God took the man and put him in the
garden of Eden to work it and keep it. ¹⁶ And
the Lord God commanded the man, saying,
'You may surely eat of every tree of the garden,
¹⁷ but of the tree of the knowledge of good and
evil you shall not eat, for in the day that you eat
of it you shall surely die.'
¹⁸ Then the Lord God said, 'It is not good that
the man should be alone; I will make him a
helper fit for him.' ¹⁹ So out of the ground the
Lord God formed every beast of the field and
every bird of the heavens and brought them to
the man to see what he would call them. And
whatever the man called every living creature,*

that was its name. [20] *The man gave names to all livestock and to the birds of the heavens and to every beast of the field. But for Adam there was not found a helper fit for him.* [21] *So the* LORD *God caused a deep sleep to fall upon the man, and while he slept took one of his ribs and closed up its place with flesh.* [22] *And the rib that the* LORD *God had taken from the man he made into a woman and brought her to the man.* [23] *Then the man said, 'This at last is bone of my bones and flesh of my flesh; she shall be called Woman, because she was taken out of Man.'* [24] *Therefore a man shall leave his father and his mother and hold fast to his wife, and they shall become one flesh.* [25] *And the man and his wife were both naked and were not ashamed.*

[3:1] *Now the serpent was more crafty than any other beast of the field that the* LORD *God had made. He said to the woman, 'Did God actually say, "You shall not eat of any tree in the garden'?"'* [2] *And the woman said to the serpent, 'We may eat of the fruit of the trees in the garden,* [3] *but God said, "You shall not eat of the fruit of the tree that is in the midst of the garden, neither shall you touch it, lest you die."'* [4] *But the serpent said to the woman, 'You will not surely die.* [5] *For God knows that when you eat of it your eyes will be opened, and you will be like God, knowing good and evil.'* [6] *So when the woman saw that the tree was good for food, and that it was a delight to the eyes, and that the tree was to be desired to make one wise, she took of its fruit and ate, and she also gave some to her husband who was with her, and he ate.* [7] *Then the eyes of both were opened, and they knew that they were naked. And they sewed fig leaves together and made themselves loincloths.*

[8] *And they heard the sound of the* Lord *God walking in the garden in the cool of the day, and the man and his wife hid themselves from the presence of the* Lord *God among the trees of the garden.* [9] *But the* Lord *God called to the man and said to him, 'Where are you?'* [10] *And he said, 'I heard the sound of you in the garden, and I was afraid, because I was naked, and I hid myself.'* [11] *He said, 'Who told you that you were naked? Have you eaten of the tree of which I commanded you not to eat?'* [12] *The man said, 'The woman whom you gave to be with me, she gave me fruit of the tree, and I ate.'* [13] *Then the* Lord *God said to the woman, 'What is this that*

you have done?' The woman said, 'The serpent deceived me, and I ate.'

[14] The LORD *God said to the serpent, 'Because you have done this, cursed are you above all livestock and above all beasts of the field; on your belly you shall go, and dust you shall eat all the days of your life.*

[15] I will put enmity between you and the woman, and between your offspring and her offspring; he shall bruise your head, and you shall bruise his heel.'

[16] To the woman he said, "I will surely multiply your pain in childbearing; in pain you shall bring forth children. Your desire shall be for your husband, and he shall rule over you.'

[17] And to Adam he said, "Because you have listened to the voice of your wife and have eaten of the tree of which I commanded you, "You shall not eat of it", cursed is the ground because of you; in pain you shall eat of it all the days of your life; [18] thorns and thistles it shall bring forth for you; and you shall eat the plants of the field. [19] By the sweat of your face you shall eat bread, till you return to the ground, for out of it you were taken; for you are dust, and to dust you shall return."'

²⁰ *The man called his wife's name Eve, because she was the mother of all living.* ²¹ *And the* LORD *God made for Adam and for his wife garments of skins and clothed them.*

²² *Then the* LORD *God said, 'Behold, the man has become like one of us in knowing good and evil. Now, lest he reach out his hand and take also of the tree of life and eat, and live forever—'* ²³ *therefore the* LORD *God sent him out from the garden of Eden to work the ground from which he was taken.* ²⁴ *He drove out the man, and at the east of the garden of Eden he placed the cherubim and a flaming sword that turned every way to guard the way to the tree of life*

(Gen. 2:15–3:24).

Had we known no guilt, we would
have known no grief.

MATTHEW HENRY

OUTLINE

*T*he implications of the theory of evolution are
not confined to the realms of natural science

– they influence every aspect of human life, including suffering. In the evolutionary framework, suffering is seen as natural, part of the essential make-up of life. If there is any hope of its elimination, that hope rests wholly on scientific progress.

Turning from the wisdom of man to the wisdom of God, we see in the Bible a far more startling explanation of the origins of suffering, together with a far more thrilling view of its certain eradication. According to Scripture, the world in its original state was a 'suffering-free zone'. It was 'very good' (*Gen.* 1:31). In the light of that, we might well say that health is the 'natural' order of things. It was the disobedience of Adam, the God-appointed head and representative of the human race, that brought the execution of the 'death penalty' upon the entire human family. Since the Fall of man in Adam, and God's punishment of him, change and decay, disease and death, have entered the world – adversely affecting both mankind and his environment. Although suffering is often aggravated by various 'sins', its fundamental cause is 'sin' itself.

This truth revealed in Scripture, however contrary to the empty despair of evolutionary teaching, actually sets the stage for an astonishing hope. For if sin were to be removed, suffering would necessarily disappear with it; suffering receives its death-blow when its *raison d'être* is taken away. This hope, as we shall see, is realized in two mighty historical events. Sin received its first body blow when Jesus Christ, the 'last Adam', the Son of God made man, cancelled its penalty of death and broke its reigning power by his death and resurrection. The benefits and power of his great work, performed as our God-appointed Representative, are communicated to us through our faith-union with him. From that moment forward, history has been moving towards the day of his return, that great day when all those justified by faith in him, will finally be conformed to his perfect, sin-free and holy likeness, and when not one of them will ever say again 'I am sick' (*Isa.* 33:24).

QUESTIONS

1. What clues are there in Genesis 1:31 and 3:16–19 that the sufferings which we regard as 'normal' were not in fact present in the world as it was originally created? How do we find this 'abnormality' psychologically confirmed in our attitudes and reactions to suffering and death?

2. If suffering is the fruit of sin, why is it logical to assume that Jesus' work on earth carries in it the

seeds of suffering's destruction (see *1 John* 3:5, 8; *Isa.* 53:5)?

3. According to Genesis 3:17–19, what other 'abnormalities' have their roots in mankind's rebellion against God, and can likewise look forward to a restoration to normality when sin is finally eliminated? (see *Rom.* 8:20–22).

3

SUFFERING AND THE SOVEREIGNTY OF GOD

There was a man in the land of Uz whose name was Job, and that man was blameless and upright, one who feared God and turned away from evil. ² *There were born to him seven sons and three daughters.* ³ *He possessed 7,000 sheep, 3,000 camels, 500 yoke of oxen, and 500 female donkeys, and very many servants, so that this man was the greatest of all the people of the east.* ⁴ *His sons used to go and hold a feast in the house of each one on his day, and they would send and invite their three sisters to eat and drink with them.* ⁵ *And when the days of the feast had run their course, Job would send and consecrate them, and he would rise early in the morning and offer burnt offerings according to the number of them all. For Job said, 'It may be that my children have sinned, and cursed God in their hearts.' Thus Job did continually.*

⁶ Now there was a day when the sons of God came to present themselves before the LORD, and Satan also came among them. ⁷ The LORD said to Satan, 'From where have you come?' Satan answered the LORD and said, 'From going to and fro on the earth, and from walking up and down on it.' ⁸ And the LORD said to Satan, 'Have you considered my servant Job, that there is none like him on the earth, a blameless and upright man, who fears God and turns away from evil?' ⁹ Then Satan answered the LORD and said, 'Does Job fear God for no reason? ¹⁰ Have you not put a hedge around him and his house and all that he has, on every side? You have blessed the work of his hands, and his possessions have increased in the land. ¹¹ But stretch out your hand and touch all that he has, and he will curse you to your face.' ¹² And the LORD said to Satan, 'Behold, all that he has is in your hand. Only against him do not stretch out your hand.' So Satan went out from the presence of the LORD.

¹³ Now there was a day when his sons and daughters were eating and drinking wine in their oldest brother's house, ¹⁴ and there came a messenger to Job and said, 'The oxen were ploughing and the donkeys feeding beside them, ¹⁵ and the Sabeans fell upon them and took them and struck down the servants with the edge of the sword, and I alone have escaped to tell you.' ¹⁶ While he was yet speaking, there came another and said, 'The fire of God fell from heaven and burned up the sheep and the servants and consumed them, and I alone have escaped to tell you.' ¹⁷ While he was yet speaking, there came another and said, 'The Chaldeans formed three groups and made a raid on the camels and took them and struck down the servants with the edge of the sword, and I alone have escaped to tell you.' ¹⁸ While he was yet speaking, there came another and said, 'Your sons and daughters were eating and drinking wine in their oldest brother's house, ¹⁹ and behold, a great wind came across the wilderness and struck the four corners of the house, and it fell upon the young people, and they are dead, and I alone have escaped to tell you.'

²⁰ Then Job arose and tore his robe and shaved his head and fell on the ground and worshipped. ²¹ And he said, 'Naked I came from my mother's womb, and naked shall I return. The Lord gave, and the Lord has taken away; blessed be the name of the Lord.' ²² In all this Job did not sin or charge God with wrong.

²:¹ Again there was a day when the sons of God came to present themselves before the Lord, and Satan also came among them to present himself before the Lord. ² And the Lord said to Satan, 'From where have you come?' Satan answered the Lord and said, 'From going to and fro on the earth, and from walking up and down on it.' ³ And the Lord said to Satan, 'Have you considered my servant Job, that there is none like him on the earth, a blameless and upright man, who fears God and turns away from evil? He still holds fast his integrity, although you incited me against him to destroy him without reason.' ⁴ Then Satan answered the Lord and said, 'Skin for skin! All that a man has he will give for his life. ⁵ But stretch out your hand and touch his bone and his flesh, and he will curse you to your face.' ⁶ And the Lord said to Satan, 'Behold, he is in your hand; only spare his life.'

⁷ So Satan went out from the presence of the LORD *and struck Job with loathsome sores from the sole of his foot to the crown of his head. ⁸ And he took a piece of broken pottery with which to scrape himself while he sat in the ashes.*

⁹ Then his wife said to him, 'Do you still hold fast your integrity? Curse God and die.' ¹⁰ But he said to her, 'You speak as one of the foolish women would speak. Shall we receive good from God, and shall we not receive evil?' In all this Job did not sin with his lips (Job 1:1–2:10).

It would destroy the confidence of God's people, could they be persuaded that God does not foreordain whatsoever comes to pass.

CHARLES HODGE

OUTLINE

*T*he modern world has not lagged behind previous generations in its propensity to think of God as it would like him to be. Amongst the varied idols produced by contemporary religious thought, the most popular is perhaps the 'God' of sentimentality who masquerades as 'love'. He is a God (it is assumed) who could not possibly be responsible for suffering.

This first assumption however leads necessarily to another – that this 'God', whose primary purpose is to serve men, is not the omnipotent God of the Bible. Indeed, taking note of the pervasive nature of suffering in the world, this God clearly has a hard time coping with the power of 'evil'. This way of thinking first appeared in the ancient heresy of Manicheism. The Manichees believed that God and Satan are locked together in equal combat, neither being strong enough to finally conquer the other. This teaching is of course flatly contradicted in the Bible. The true perspective as revealed in Holy Scripture is altogether more robust and reassuring.

It is the unanimous testimony of Scripture that God is God — even when suffering stalks this world; even, we might add, in cases where that suffering appears 'unmerited'. Job is perhaps the clearest example of this Scripture truth. At no point in his trials is Job ever in doubt as to the absolute sovereignty of God over his personal circumstances. What causes his perplexity is not God's power, but (under the pressure of the misapplied reasoning of his 'comforters')

God's justice. Satan's role in the whole affair is purely subordinate and instrumental. Significantly, Satan does not even warrant a mention after the close of Chapter 2.

Of course, this does not solve the mystery as to why the righteous suffer, but it does lay down very important guidelines for an informed approach to suffering. What is more, if God is sovereign over suffering, then the first and wisest move for any sufferer is to cast himself wholly on God.

QUESTIONS

1. How is God's sovereignty over human suffering demonstrated in the events of Job 1–2, and especially in the reactions of Job himself to his suffering?

2. How extensive is God's sovereignty over suffering, according to Exodus 4:11? What dignity does the content of this biblical statement give to people who might otherwise be overlooked, discriminated against, or even disposed of in the womb?

3. What comfort should the truth of God's omnipotence be to the godly who suffer (see *Matt.* 10:29–31; *1 Cor.* 10:13)?

4

SUFFERING AND THE JUSTICE OF GOD

And the LORD said to Job: ² *'Shall a fault-finder contend with the Almighty? He who argues with God, let him answer it.'*

³ *Then Job answered the LORD and said:* ⁴ *'Behold, I am of small account; what shall I answer you? I lay my hand on my mouth.* ⁵ *I have spoken once, and I will not answer; twice, but I will proceed no further.'*

⁶ *Then the LORD answered Job out of the whirlwind and said:* ⁷ *'Dress for action like a man; I will question you, and you make it known to me.* ⁸ *Will you even put me in the wrong? Will you condemn me that you may be in the right?* ⁹ *Have you an arm like God, and can you thunder with a voice like his?* ¹⁰ *Adorn yourself*

with majesty and dignity; clothe yourself with glory and splendour. [11] Pour out the overflowings of your anger, and look on everyone who is proud and abase him. [12] Look on everyone who is proud and bring him low and tread down the wicked where they stand. [13] Hide them all in the dust together; bind their faces in the world below. [14] Then will I also acknowledge to you that your own right hand can save you.

[15] Behold, Behemoth, which I made as I made you; he eats grass like an ox. [16] Behold, his strength in his loins, and his power in the muscles of his belly. [17] He makes his tail stiff like a cedar; the sinews of his thighs are knit together. [18] His bones are tubes of bronze, his limbs like bars of iron. [19] He is the first of the works of God; let him who made him bring near his sword! [20] For the mountains yield food for him where all the wild beasts play. [21] Under the lotus plants he lies, in the shelter of the reeds and in the marsh. [22] For his shade the lotus trees cover him; the willows of the brook surround him. [23] Behold, if the river is turbulent he is not frightened; he is confident though Jordan rushes against his mouth. [24] Can one take him by his eyes, or pierce his nose with a snare?

41:1 Can you draw out Leviathan with a fish-hook or press down his tongue with a cord? 2 Can you put a rope in his nose or pierce his jaw with a hook? 3 Will he make many pleas to you? Will he speak to you soft words? 4 Will he make a covenant with you to take him for your servant forever? 5 Will you play with him as with a bird, or will you put him on a leash for your girls? 6 Will traders bargain over him? Will they divide him up among the merchants? 7 Can you fill his skin with harpoons or his head with fishing spears? 8 Lay your hands on him; remember the battle – you will not do it again! 9 Behold, the hope of a man is false; he is laid low even at the sight of him. 10 No one is so fierce that he dares to stir him up. Who then is he who can stand before me? 11 Who has first given to me, that I should repay him? Whatever is under the whole heaven is mine. 12 I will not keep silence concerning his limbs, or his mighty strength, or his goodly frame. 13 Who can strip off his outer garment? Who would come near him with a bridle? 14 Who can open the doors of his face? Around his teeth is terror. 15 His back is made of rows of shields, shut up closely as with a seal. 16 One is so near to another that no air can come between them. [17] They are joined one to another; they clasp each other and cannot be separated. [18] His sneezings flash forth light, and his eyes are like the eyelids of the dawn. [19] Out of his mouth go flaming torches; sparks of fire leap forth. [20] Out of his nostrils comes forth smoke, as from a boiling pot and burning rushes. [21] His breath kindles coals, and a flame comes forth from his mouth. [22] In his neck abides strength, and terror dances before him. [23] The folds of his flesh stick together, firmly cast on him and immovable. [24] His heart is hard as a stone, hard as the lower millstone. [25] When he raises himself up the mighty are afraid; at the crashing they are beside themselves. [26] Though the sword reaches him, it does not avail, nor the spear, the dart, or the javelin. [27] He counts iron as straw, and bronze as rotten wood. [28] The arrow cannot make him flee; for him sling stones are turned to stubble. [29] Clubs are counted as stubble; he laughs at the rattle of javelins. [30] His underparts are like sharp potsherds; he spreads himself like a threshing sledge on the mire. [31] He makes the deep boil like a pot; he makes the sea like a pot of ointment. [32] Behind him he leaves a shining wake; one would think *the deep to be white-haired.* [33] *On earth there is not his like, a creature without fear.* [34] *He sees everything that is high; he is king over all the sons of pride.'*

[42:1] *Then Job answered the LORD and said:* [2] *'I know that you can do all things, and that no purpose of yours can be thwarted.* [3] *"Who is this that hides counsel without knowledge?" Therefore I have uttered what I did not understand, things too wonderful for me, which I did not know.* [4] *"Hear, and I will speak; I will question you, and you make it known to me."* [5] *I had heard of you by the hearing of the ear, but now my eye sees you;* [6] *therefore I despise myself, and repent in dust and ashes'* (*Job* 40:1–42:6).

If he had utterly forsaken the whole race of mankind . . . and left them all as remediless as the fallen angels, there could have been no reflection on his goodness.

JOHN OWEN

OUTLINE

*N*owhere more, perhaps, than in considering the relationship between suffering and divine justice are we to allow Scripture rather than our own opinions to dictate and guide us. And that for a very simple reason – our perspectives are instinctively skewed. For if there is one characteristic that marks us all, it is self-righteousness – that over-estimate of our own goodness, flowing from our under-estimation of the holiness of God. It is a characteristic that can only be broken by the 'convicting' work of the Holy Spirit (see *John* 16:8), bringing us face-to-face with God as he really is in Christ. For, living as we all do in the ever-present smog of a sin-laden environment, we find it impossible to appreciate the vileness of our own ungodliness until we are confronted by the shocking revelation of God himself (see the reactions of Isaiah, Peter, and John to such a confrontation: *Isa.* 6:1–5; *Luke* 5:1–8; *Rev.* 1:12–17). Sin, even in what we might consider its milder forms, is an abomination to God; he hates it and has decreed that every case of sin is deserving of death. After all, just one sin brought the entire human race into condemnation at the hands of the

28

God who always acts justly in keeping with his just and righteous being. And yet, according to God's own verdict, all the ways of every man are marked with this ugly stain.

Job's history serves to prove the point in dramatic fashion. Here is a 'righteous' man, if ever there was one (see *Ezek.*14:14, for further confirmation). If any man deserved to be rewarded and blessed it was surely him. Yet he is afflicted – even to the point where he questions the justice of God towards him and cries out in self-vindication. Yet, even Job, when once exposed to the God of holiness, is silenced and brought to self-emptying repentance. The teaching of the Bible is that if justice was strictly enforced, unconditioned by grace, no-one would survive the ordeal (*Psa.* 130:3).

QUESTIONS

1. Why is Job's repentance at the end of the book so significant when seen in the light of Job 1:1–5?

2. In the light of the divine verdict on the entire human race in Romans 3:9–20, why is it inaccurate to speak of 'innocent suffering'? What is the real

state of affairs as explained by Ezra 9:13 and Psalm 103:10?

3. What does the fact that there will be no grounds for appeal against the divine sentence on the day of judgment mean for this whole question (see *Job* 9:2–3; *Rom.*3:19)?

5

THE MYSTERY
OF SUFFERING

Truly God is good to Israel, to those who are pure in heart. *2 But as for me, my feet had almost stumbled, my steps had nearly slipped. *3 For I was envious of the arrogant when I saw the prosperity of the wicked.* *4 For they have no pangs until death; their bodies are fat and sleek.* *5 They are not in trouble as others are; they are not stricken like the rest of mankind.* *6 Therefore pride is their necklace; violence covers them as a garment.* *7 Their eyes swell out through fatness; their hearts overflow with follies.* *8 They scoff and speak with malice; loftily they threaten oppression.* *9 They set their mouths against the heavens, and their tongue struts through the earth.* *10 Therefore his people turn back to them,* *and find no fault in them.* [11] *And they say, 'How can God know? Is there knowledge in the Most High?'* [12] *Behold, these are the wicked; always at ease, they increase in riches.* [13] *All in vain have I kept my heart clean and washed my hands in innocence.* [14] *For all the day long I have been stricken and rebuked every morning.* [15] *If I had said, 'I will speak thus', I would have betrayed the generation of your children.* [16] *But when I thought how to understand this, it seemed to me a wearisome task,* [17] *until I went into the sanctuary of God; then I discerned their end.* [18] *Truly you set them in slippery places; you make them fall to ruin.* [19] *How they are destroyed in a moment, swept away utterly by terrors!* [20] *Like a dream when one awakes, O Lord, when you rouse yourself, you despise them as phantoms.* [21] *When my soul was embittered, when I was pricked in heart,* [22] *I was brutish and ignorant; I was like a beast toward you.* [23] *Nevertheless, I am continually with you; you hold my right hand.* [24] *You guide me with your counsel, and afterward you will receive me to glory.* [25] *Whom have I in heaven but you? And there is nothing on earth that I desire besides you.* [26] *My flesh and my heart may fail, but God is the strength of my heart and my portion for ever.* ²⁷ *For behold, those who are far from you shall perish; you put an end to everyone who is unfaithful to you.* ²⁸ *But for me it is good to be near God; I have made the Lord GOD my refuge, that I may tell of all your works* (*Psa.* 73).

> He deserves the hottest hell, but
> has the warmest nest.
>
> CHARLES SPURGEON
> (*commenting on the
> prosperity of the wicked*)

OUTLINE

*T*he 'Wisdom books' of the Old Testament should cause us to pause before rushing to hasty 'cause-and-effect' conclusions on the reasons why we or anyone else experiences a particular form of suffering. For where the book of Proverbs presents us with observations concerning the general fact of the blessedness of the righteous and the woes of the wicked, the exceptions to the general rule are numerous enough to warrant the inclusion of the books of Job and Ecclesiastes in the canon of Scripture. The former charts the extreme afflictions of a godly man, whilst the latter reflects on the impossibility of 'cracking the code' of the providential mysteries of life on earth (see *Eccles.* 8:14). Both books bear testimony to the reality that there are times when suffering appears to be arbitrary in its choice of victim. The seemingly illogical nature of so much suffering, and the perplexity it causes in our minds, are the unavoidable result of three fundamental facts – the hiddeness of God's being and ways; the disorder brought into the universe by the entrance of sin; and our own sin-induced inability as fallen creatures to see things as they really are. This element of mystery is reinforced in the teaching of the Lord Jesus Christ (see *Luke* 13:1–5; *John* 9:1–3). Although there would be no suffering in the world had 'sin' not entered into it, it is an altogether more complex puzzle to discover the exact relationship between suffering and our own 'sins'. Psalm 73 is perhaps the classic treatment of this perplexing problem in Scripture – a problem whose perplexities will only be resolved in eternity.

QUESTIONS

1. What is the over-riding certainty which governs the Psalmist's consideration of the problem

of suffering in this psalm? (see *Psa.* 73:1). For all that we lack or suffer from, what do we possess in Christ that outweighs such sufferings? (see 1 *Cor.* 3:21–23).

2. What caused the writer such anguish, according to Psalm 73:2–15? Even if this was the whole story (which it is not),what 'inner' blessings do the wicked who prosper lack even at the height of their prosperity (see *Isa.* 48:22)?

3. What perspective does the writer of this psalm find it necessary to adopt in order to see clearly in the midst of this confusion (see *Psa.* 73:16–22)?

6

SIN AND SUFFERING

If you are not careful to do all the words of this law that are written in this book, that you may fear this glorious and awesome name, the Lord *your God,* [59] *then the* Lord *will bring on you and your offspring extraordinary afflictions, afflictions severe and lasting, and sicknesses grievous and lasting.* [60] *And he will bring upon you again all the diseases of Egypt, of which you were afraid, and they shall cling to you.* [61] *Every sickness also and every affliction that is not recorded in the book of this law, the* Lord *will bring upon you, until you are destroyed.* [62] *Whereas you were as numerous as the stars*

of heaven, you shall be left few in number, because you did not obey the voice of the LORD
your God. [63] And as the LORD took delight in
doing you good and multiplying you, so the
LORD will take delight in bringing ruin upon
you and destroying you. And you shall be
plucked off the land that you are entering to
take possession of it.

[64] And the LORD will scatter you among all
peoples, from one end of the earth to the other,
and there you shall serve other gods of wood
and stone, which neither you nor your fathers
have known. [65] And among these nations you
shall find no respite, and there shall be no
resting place for the sole of your foot, but the
LORD will give you there a trembling heart and
failing eyes and a languishing soul. [66] Your life
shall hang in doubt before you. Night and day
you shall be in dread and have no assurance
of your life. [67] In the morning you shall say,
'If only it were evening!' and at evening you
shall say, 'If only it were morning!' because
of the dread that your heart shall feel, and the
sights that your eyes shall see. [68] And the LORD
will bring you back in ships to Egypt, a journey
that I promised that you should never make

again; and there you shall offer yourselves for sale to your enemies as male and female slaves, but there will be no buyer (Deut. 28: 58–68).

Whoever, therefore, eats the bread or drinks the cup of the Lord in an unworthy manner will be guilty of profaning the body and blood of the Lord. [28] Let a person examine himself, then, and so eat of the bread and drink of the cup. [29] For anyone who eats and drinks without discerning the body eats and drinks judgment on himself. [30] That is why many of you are weak and ill, and some have died. [31] But if we judged ourselves truly, we would not be judged. [32] But when we are judged by the Lord, we are disciplined so that we may not be condemned along with the world (1 Cor. 11:27–32).

Pain gives the only opportunity the bad man can have for amendment. It removes the veil; it plants the flag of truth within the fortress of a rebel soul.

C. S. Lewis

OUTLINE

One of the dangers we face in thinking about the question of suffering is that of running to extremes. One such extreme would be to conclude, for example, in the light of the first half of Psalm 73, that suffering is totally inexplicable in its individual manifestation and experience. For just as the teaching of the book of Proverbs needs to be set alongside the book of Ecclesiastes (see *Outline* comments in Study 5), so the opposite is also true. That there is mystery in men's experience of health and suffering, blessing and misfortune, is axiomatic (see *Jer.* 12:1; *Job* 12:6). That this is the only strand of biblical teaching on the subject is simply not the case.

The book of Proverbs speaks unambiguously both about the health-giving benefits of a well-ordered, God-fearing life (see *Prov.* 3:5–8), and the painful side-effects of living without God's wisdom (see *Prov.* 13:21). Its clear message is that sin does not pay – not even on this side of the grave. What is more, the two passages under consideration prove that the Lord employs suffering as corrective discipline in order to bring his wayward children to their senses and to further their growth in holiness. Whether it is a case of dealing with Old Testament Israel in her covenant-breaking lawlessness, or members of the church in first-century Corinth, whose actions regarding the Lord's Supper injured the members of Christ's body, God uses the rod of chastisement to correct sinful behaviour.

The fact that this element may be present in our sufferings makes self-examination one of our first duties in any Christian response to the onset of affliction.

QUESTIONS

1. How do these two passages undermine the idea that all sickness is necessarily inexplicable, arbitrary, or simply and exclusively satanic? Whose hand is behind the sufferings of God's people in the two cases cited, and why?

2. What evidence is there in Deuteronomy 30:1–10 that the afflictions of Deuteronomy 28 had, in God's hands, a constructive and not a destructive purpose (see also *1 Cor.* 11:27–32; Job 33:14–30)?

3. What should form part of our reaction to suffering according to James 5:14–20? Why is this a good

thing to do even if, unknown to us, there exists no necessary link between our suffering and a particular sin? (see Psa. 139:23-24).

7

THE SUPREME SUFFERER

Since then we have a great high priest who has passed through the heavens, Jesus, the Son of God, let us hold fast our confession. [15] *For we do not have a high priest who is unable to sympathize with our weaknesses, but one who in every respect has been tempted as we are, yet without sin.* [16] *Let us then with confidence draw near to the throne of grace, that we may receive mercy and find grace to help in time of need.* [5:1] *For every high priest chosen from among men is appointed to act on behalf of men in relation to God, to offer gifts and sacrifices for sins.* [2] *He can deal gently with the ignorant and wayward, since he himself is beset with weakness.*

³ Because of this he is bound to offer sacrifice for his own sins just as he does for those of the people. ⁴ And no one takes this honour for himself, but only when called by God, just as Aaron was.

⁵ So also Christ did not exalt himself to be made a high priest, but was appointed by him who said to him, 'You are my Son, today I have begotten you'; ⁶ as he says also in another place, 'You are a priest forever, after the order of Melchizedek.'

⁷ In the days of his flesh, Jesus offered up prayers and supplications, with loud cries and tears, to him who was able to save him from death, and he was heard because of his reverence. ⁸ Although he was a son, he learned obedience through what he suffered. ⁹ And being made perfect, he became the source of eternal salvation to all who obey him, ¹⁰ being designated by God a high priest after the order of Melchizedek (Heb. 4:14–5:10).

He suffered in his soul the dreadful torments of a person condemned and irretrievably lost.

JOHN CALVIN

OUTLINE

*N*o consideration of suffering is complete without a reflection on the sufferings of the Lord Jesus Christ. For here is suffering at its zenith. In the first place, Jesus' sufferings were constant. He was, in Isaiah's words, 'a man of sorrows, and acquainted with grief ' (*Isa.* 53:3). His life was, in one writer's estimation, 'a perpetual Gethsemane'. Unlike us, whose natural instincts and inclinations veer towards the corrupting and defiling, he in his innate, perfect innocence suffered through his daily exposure to sin and its effects. Unlike other men, when he experienced temptation (as he had to do in order to qualify as our true Representative and High Priest), he suffered.

But then secondly, the sufferings of the incarnate Son of God were of a unique character and intensity. His whole life was lived in the shadow of the cross. A form of death horrible enough in itself, but made all the more unthinkable by the fact that in his case, the cross was to be the place of experiencing the divine curse (see *Deut.* 21:23; *Gal.* 3:13); the place where the undiluted wrath of an avenging God against guilty sinners was concentrated in the body and soul of a

45

single, solitary, abandoned man. Who can possibly begin to grasp the soul's desolation contained in the words Jesus cried from the cross: 'My God, my God! Why have you forsaken me?' To even anticipate that experience was enough to make his sweat 'like great drops of blood falling down to the ground' (*Luke* 22:44). The depths of the physical, psychological, and spiritual sufferings of our Saviour are simply unfathomable.

The importance of all this to the Christian is not confined to the glorious truth that by his sufferings, Jesus was sealing the death of human woe by cancelling our sin, which is the ultimate cause of all our woes. Nor is the significance of what he endured merely that of a wonderful example. Rather, according to our Scripture passage, it is that such sufferings have equipped Jesus to act as our High Priest who, because of what he has personally experienced, understands our every sorrow, and as the omnipresent, omnipotent God, is able to provide not just sympathy but very real help.

QUESTIONS

1. Consider the extent of the Lord Jesus' sufferings referred to in Hebrews 5:8 and described in

Luke 22:9–44; 63–65; 23:6–46. Can ours compare with this?

2. What was the most painful element in Jesus' sufferings according to Isaiah 53:5–6, 10? What encouragement should it be to us that we will never be in the situation on this earth that he occupied in Matthew 27:46?

3. If, as Hebrews 4:15 suggests, the Lord Jesus can accurately be described as one

> *who every grief has known*
> *that wrings the human breast,*

what should we be encouraged to do in our sufferings, according to Hebrews 4:16? What kind of reception should we expect (see *Heb.* 2:17–18)?

8

HEALING AND
SUFFERING

For I consider that the sufferings of this present time are not worth comparing with the glory that is to be revealed to us. [19] For the creation waits with eager longing for the revealing of the sons of God. [20] For the creation was subjected to futility, not willingly, but because of him who subjected it, in hope [21] that the creation itself will be set free from its bondage to decay and obtain the freedom of the glory of the children of God. [22] For we know that the whole creation has been groaning together in the pains of childbirth until now. [23] And not only the creation, but we ourselves, who have the firstfruits of the Spirit, groan inwardly as we wait eagerly for adoption

*as sons, the redemption of our bodies. ²⁴ For in
this hope we were saved. Now hope that is seen
is not hope. For who hopes for what he sees?
²⁵ But if we hope for what we do not see, we
wait for it with patience (Rom. 8:18–25).*

The body is not yet saved.

D. MARTYN LLOYD-JONES

OUTLINE

*I*t is a foundational biblical truth that our daily
survival as well as our continuing 'quality of life'
are entirely dependent on God's ongoing, sustaining
grace. Good health is his unmerited gift, a visible
proof that he has been pleased not to stir up his full
anger against our rebellious race. Such grace finds it
source in God's goodness, whether mediated through
miracle or medicine. It is therefore sinful blindness to
look to doctors for help without looking simultane-
ously and supremely to God himself (see 2 *Chron.*
16:12). This divine grace comes to its full expression,
of course, in the gospel, a message of good news for
man in the entirety of his body/soul constitution.

Because Jesus has died, and the root cause of all our ills has been removed in his propitiation for sin, the legal basis has been established for the eventual elimination of all suffering and woe for the Christian believer. The passage under consideration however, reveals something crucial – that despite the breaking-in of God's kingdom into this fallen world, there is a 'not yet' as well as a 'here-and-now' aspect to the fruits of Jesus Christ's work. For just as sin remains an active force in spite of its 'legal' defeat, so its off-spring of suffering continues in existence for a time, although doomed to destruction one day. The healing miracles of Jesus and his apostles are to be regarded not only as 'signs' which authenticated their calling and message, but as harbingers of that which is yet to be when the King comes again to consummate his eternal kingdom in the new heavens and new earth. The many miracles of Jesus and his apostles, which took place in the brief years of the New Testament era, are not to be seen as examples of what can be enjoyed by all in the here-and-now.

It is within this context that the delicate issue of healing needs to be approached. Contrary to the teaching of those who like Hymenaeus and Philetus claim that the 'resurrection has already taken place' (see 2 *Tim.* 2:17-18), the salvation of the body lies still in the future. While instances of divine healing may be experienced on occasion, they are usually exceptional and necessarily partial. The fullness of our salvation is inextricably bound to 'our blessed hope, the appearing of the glory of our great God and Saviour Jesus Christ' (*Titus* 2:13).

QUESTIONS

1. What indications do we find in the passage that the redemption of our bodies is reserved for the future? Why does this fact in no way detract from its attraction? (see *Rom.* 8:18; 2 *Cor.* 4:17).

2. How do Jesus' dealings with the paralysed man of Mark 2:1–12 demonstrate the priority at the present time of the forgiveness of men's sins over the healing of men's sicknesses?

3. What guidelines are we given in James 5:13–20 for seeking physical restoration? What further light is shed on this matter by Paul's praying in 2 Corinthians 12:7–9, in particular, concerning the persistence in such prayer in the light of God's 'No' or 'Not yet'?

9

A GREATER SUFFERING

Whoever causes one of these little ones who believe in me to sin, it would be better for him if a great millstone were hung around his neck and he were thrown into the sea. ⁴³ And if your hand causes you to sin, cut it off. It is better for you to enter life crippled than with two hands to go to hell, to the unquenchable fire. ⁴⁴ And if your foot causes you to sin, cut it off. It is better for you to enter life lame than with two feet to be thrown into hell. ⁴⁵ And if your eye causes you to sin, tear it out. It is better for you to enter the kingdom of God with one eye than with two eyes to be thrown into hell, ⁴⁶ 'where their worm does not die and the fire is not quenched.' [49] For everyone will be salted with fire. [50] Salt is good, but if the salt has lost its saltiness, how will you make it salty again? Have salt in yourselves, and be at peace with one another (Mark 9:42–50).

The damned shall suffer an end without end; a death without death; a decay without decay . . . they shall have a punishment without pity; misery without mercy; sorrow without succour; crying without comfort; torment without ease.

JOHN CHRYSOSTOM

OUTLINE

*B*ecause biblical truth forms an integrated whole, if one element in it is discarded, there is an inevitable undermining of the rest. Over the last century or so, we have seen this process at work in various directions, not least in the 'side-effects' accompanying the dilution of the Bible's revelation of God's true character. Alongside the reduction of God's love to a benign sentimentality, the abolition of the truth of God's wrath against sin, the Bible's teaching about hell has been sanitized, if not totally eliminated. With the removal of this biblical framework, in which eternal concerns outweigh those of this visible world (and in particular of the threat of everlasting punishment and suffering), we find ourselves in a culture in which people are preoccupied only with the present. God's truth is not, however, subject to repeal by the changing fashions in popular thinking. And it comes as something of a shock to modern men and women, who are accustomed to the materialistic, pleasure-seeking atmosphere of our contemporary world and whose outlook on life is totally earth-bound, to enter the world of Scripture – a world in which the present order of things is transient, 'passing away'; a world where the only thing that really counts is eternity.

In this latter world (which is the *real* 'real world'), hell is a truly awful reality. Spoken of by the Lord Jesus himself far more than by any other character in Scripture, hell's importance in terms of our understanding of suffering is huge. The biblical doctrine of hell has the impact of relativizing all our earthly sufferings by dwarfing them both in terms of their intensity and duration. The solemn fact of hell's existence ought to have the effect of transforming our priorities and replacing health with holiness at the top of our agenda.

QUESTIONS

1. What implications do the Lord Jesus Christ's words in Mark 9:42–50 have for the popular modern belief that 'good health is everything'?

2. What kinds of behaviour and attitude, if not repented of, put people in danger of hell, according to Mark 9:42–48? (see also *Matt.* 5:27–30). On this basis, how many are in danger, and how can they escape (see Luke 13:1–5)?

3. How does Jesus' teaching in Luke 12:4–5 and Luke 16:19–31 reinforce the fact that what takes place after death makes both the pleasures and pains of earthly life pale into significance?

DIVINE PURPOSES IN SUFFERING

James, a servant of God and of the Lord Jesus Christ, To the twelve tribes in the Dispersion: Greetings.

2 Count it all joy, my brothers, when you meet trials of various kinds, 3 for you know that the testing of your faith produces steadfastness. 4 And let steadfastness have its full effect, that you may be perfect and complete, lacking in nothing.

5 If any of you lacks wisdom, let him ask God, who gives generously to all without reproach, and it will be given him. 6 But let him ask in faith, with no doubting, for the one who doubts is like a wave of the sea that is driven and tossed by the wind. 7 For that person must not suppose that he will receive anything from the Lord; [8] *he is a double-minded man, unstable in all his ways.*

[9] *Let the lowly brother boast in his exaltation,* [10] *and the rich in his humiliation, because like a flower of the grass he will pass away.* [11] *For the sun rises with its scorching heat and withers the grass; its flower falls, and its beauty perishes. So also will the rich man fade away in the midst of his pursuits.*

[12] *Blessed is the man who remains steadfast under trial, for when he has stood the test he will receive the crown of life, which God has promised to those who love him (James* 1:1–12).

The true Christian ideal is not to be
happy, but to be holy.

A. W. TOZER

OUTLINE

Once we have been set free from ideas that deny God's sovereignty in suffering, it is both logical and biblical to conclude that the all-wise God, who 'works all things according to the counsel of his will' (*Eph.* 1:11), has his own good purposes in the afflictions we suffer in this life. Though the ways of God are ultimately unsearchable, certain clear scriptural truths provide us with a 'grid reference' for understanding to some extent what God's purposes may be.

Firstly, it is an axiom of the Bible that God's supreme and rightful purpose in all things is his own glory. Lazarus suffered illness and death and his sisters experienced the agony of grief in order that God's glory might shine all the more brightly in the resurrection of the dead (see *John* 11:4).

Secondly, Scripture reveals that the eternal salvation of men and women is God's good pleasure, even if this should come at the cost of their earthly comforts. Hence the reason why so many can trace the beginnings of their repentance and coming to their spiritual senses to some life-crisis that involved suffering (see *Job* 33:14–30; *Psa.* 107:10–20).

Finally, in the case of those who have become his new-born children, God's overarching concern is their growing conformity to the character of his

Son, the Lord Jesus Christ (see *Rom.* 8:29). Once again, in pursuit of this end, the Lord proves ready to make use of suffering as a painful, but in his hands, productive tool (see also *John* 15:1–2). Indeed, even the incarnate Son, though inherently holy, is required to submit to the experience of suffering in order that he might learn obedience and to qualify him to be our compassionate and sympathetic High Priest (see *Heb.* 5:8; 4:15).

In the passage for study, the focus falls on God's refining purposes in the sufferings of those who are his own.

QUESTIONS

1. What is to be the believer's attitude to his sufferings, according to James 1:2–4? To which of his sufferings is he to adopt such an attitude? Why?

2. What vital characteristic is developed by God-appointed suffering rightly approached, according to this passage? (see also *Rom.* 5:3–5). Why is this characteristic such an important factor in proving the existence of true faith (see *Matt.* 24:13; *Heb.* 10:36–39)?

3. Consider the statements of Psalm 119:67, 71, 75. In what ways have you discovered this reality? What effect should this truth have on the way you react to future suffering?

II

STRENGTH IN SUFFERING

I must go on boasting. Though there is nothing to be gained by it, I will go on to visions and revelations of the Lord. ^{2} *I know a man in Christ who fourteen years ago was caught up to the third heaven — whether in the body or out of the body I do not know, God knows.* ^{3} *And I know that this man was caught up into paradise — whether in the body or out of the body I do not know, God knows —* ^{4} *and he heard things that cannot be told, which man may not utter.* ^{5} *On behalf of this man I will boast, but on my own behalf I will not boast, except of my weaknesses.* ^{6} *Though if I should wish to boast, I would not be a fool, for I would be speaking the truth. But I refrain from it, so that no one may think more of me than he sees in me or hears from me. ⁷ So to keep me from being too elated by the surpassing greatness of the revelations, a thorn was given me in the flesh, a messenger of Satan to harass me, to keep me from being too elated. ⁸ Three times I pleaded with the Lord about this, that it should leave me. ⁹ But he said to me, 'My grace is sufficient for you, for my power is made perfect in weakness.' Therefore I will boast all the more gladly of my weaknesses, so that the power of Christ may rest upon me. ¹⁰ For the sake of Christ, then, I am content with weaknesses, insults, hardships, persecutions, and calamities. For when I am weak, then I am strong* (2 Cor. 12:1–10).

I see grace groweth best in winter.

SAMUEL RUTHERFORD

OUTLINE

*A*ccording to God's Word a man's strength is not to be measured by anything he possesses in himself – whether muscle-power, will-power, or financial clout. Rather, because power belongs to the Lord, human strength is dependent on the extent to which a man leans on God. 'I can do all things through him who strengthens me' (*Phil.* 4:13). For in the areas that matter – the things that count for eternity – be a man ever so intelligent, imposing, qualified or gifted, he can do nothing if he is not energized by God in Christ (*John* 15:5).

However, to rid us however of that innate self-reliance, pride, vainglory, and self-confidence which render us weak, what is often required is a severe 'pruning'.

In the passage under consideration, Paul is defending the authority of his apostolic ministry in the face of the opposition coming from the so-called 'super-apostles', who were attempting to usurp his authority among the Corinthian Christians by appealing to their own 'special' credentials, which were diametrically opposed to those of Christ's true apostle, Paul. The credentials of these super-apostles consisted in the strength that sprang from human prowess. Responding to this challenge, Paul reveals how his strength lay in the power of Christ – a power that was supremely displayed in Paul's human weakness – a weakness seen most clearly in the midst of his sufferings.

Perhaps the feature of greatest significance in this passage for Christians throughout the ages is that Paul's 'thorn in the flesh' or affliction is not identified. Scripture's silence on this matter enables us to apply the lesson the Lord taught Paul to the whole varied range of our own sufferings.

QUESTIONS

1. Although it was delivered through the malicious instrumentality of Satan, who was ultimately (and most lovingly) behind Paul's 'thorn in the flesh', according to this passage? How does this truth reassure us as we try to trace the origins of our own sufferings (see *John* 18:11)?

2. What did the Lord grant to the Apostle Paul, instead of answering his request to remove his thorn? In what ways is this more important than healing?

3. What discoveries have you made of the spiritual 'advantages' of affliction, as outlined in verses 9 and 10? In what ways can good health and financial prosperity prove a threat to our spiritual health (see *Prov.* 30:7–8; *Luke* 8:14)?

12

THE HOPE OF
THE SUFFERER

For I consider that the sufferings of this present time are not worth comparing with the glory that is to be revealed to us. [19] For the creation waits with eager longing for the revealing of the sons of God. [20] For the creation was subjected to futility, not willingly, but because of him who subjected it, in hope [21] that the creation itself will be set free from its bondage to decay and obtain the freedom of the glory of the children of God. [22] For we know that the whole creation has been groaning together in the pains of childbirth until now. [23] And not only the creation, but we ourselves, who have the firstfruits of the Spirit, groan inwardly as we wait eagerly for adoption as sons, the redemption of our bodies. [24] *For in this hope we were saved. Now hope that is seen is not hope. For who hopes for what he sees?* [25] *But if we hope for what we do not see, we wait for it with patience.*

[26] *Likewise the Spirit helps us in our weakness. For we do not know what to pray for as we ought, but the Spirit himself intercedes for us with groanings too deep for words.* [27] *And he who searches hearts knows what is the mind of the Spirit, because the Spirit intercedes for the saints according to the will of God.* [28] *And we know that for those who love God all things work together for good, for those who are called according to his purpose.* [29] *For those whom he foreknew he also predestined to be conformed to the image of his Son, in order that he might be the firstborn among many brothers.* [30] *And those whom he predestined he also called, and those whom he called he also justified, and those whom he justified he also glorified.*

[31] *What then shall we say to these things? If God is for us, who can be against us?* [32] *He who did not spare his own Son but gave him up for us all, how will he not also with him graciously*

give us all things? [33] *Who shall bring any charge against God's elect? It is God who justifies.* [34] *Who is to condemn? Christ Jesus is the one who died — more than that, who was raised — who is at the right hand of God, who indeed is interceding for us.* [35] *Who shall separate us from the love of Christ? Shall tribulation, or distress, or persecution, or famine, or nakedness, or danger, or sword?* [36] *As it is written, 'For your sake we are being killed all the day long; we are regarded as sheep to be slaughtered.'* [37] *No, in all these things we are more than conquerors through him who loved us.* [38] *For I am sure that neither death nor life, nor angels nor rulers, nor things present nor things to come, nor powers,* [39] *nor height nor depth, nor anything else in all creation, will be able to separate us from the love of God in Christ Jesus our Lord* (*Rom.* 8:18–39).

The losses I wrote to your ladyship of are but summer showers that will only wet your garments for an hour or two, and the sun of the New Jerusalem shall quickly dry the wet coat.

SAMUEL RUTHERFORD

OUTLINE

*I*n spite of the many consolations known by the believer which enable him or her to endure earthly suffering, it remains the final verdict of God's Word that 'if in this life only we have hoped in Christ, we are of all people most to be pitied'(*1 Cor.* 15:19). This is why the inspired biblical writers, in motivating us to persevere, would have us fix our eyes on the glories of eternity – the 'age to come'. This, far from being the nebulous, disembodied existence of much modern religious thought, is substantial, solid, and all-encompassing. The gospel has at its heart (and not at its circumference!) the doctrine of the resurrection – of Christ and his people, and, in a sense, 'all things'.

Because this is not a 'throw-away universe' (Philip Eveson), the entire created order will participate in the restoration that will commence with the glorification of God's people at the return of our Lord and Saviour Jesus Christ. The Scriptures see this new phase of Christian existence as dwarfing both the blessings and the woes of our life on earth, in terms of both quality and quantity. It is in anticipation of this glory that the physical world, as well as those who have the firstfruits of the Spirit, 'groan'.

Richard Baxter, the seventeenth-century Puritan pastor, in his book, *The Saints' Everlasting Rest*, explains how, following a brush with death, he resolved to devote at least half an hour each day to the exercise of meditating on eternity. How good it would be if every Christian resolved to do just that! For it was contemplating the coming glory that sus-tained the Lord Jesus in his agonies (*Heb.* 12:2) and enabled the apostle Paul to 'finish his course' and 'keep the faith'. One of the key disciplines of the Christian life is to focus one's attention beyond present sufferings, on future glory.

QUESTIONS

1. What is the whole of creation waiting for, according to Romans 8:19–22 (see also James 1:18)? Consider the scope of this coming glory as described in 1 Corinthians 15:42–49; Philippians 3:20–21; Revelation 21:3–7.

2. 'Glorification' is the word theologians use to describe the full, future transformation of a Christian

into the perfect likeness of the Lord Jesus Christ. What is so significant about the fact that this is described in the past tense in Romans 8:29–30? What guarantee of future glory do we have within ourselves according to Romans 8:9–11?

3. In the light of these facts, what are we exhorted to do on a continual basis in Colossians 3:1–4? What does this involve in practice?

13

PERSPECTIVES ON SUFFERING

Therefore, since we are surrounded by so great a cloud of witnesses, let us also lay aside every weight, and sin which clings so closely, and let us run with endurance the race that is set before us, [2] looking to Jesus, the founder and perfecter of our faith, who for the joy that was set before him endured the cross, despising the shame, and is seated at the right hand of the throne of God.

[3] Consider him who endured from sinners such hostility against himself, so that you may not grow weary or fainthearted. [4] In your struggle against sin you have not yet resisted to the point of shedding your blood. [5] And have you forgotten the exhortation that addresses you as sons?

'My son, do not regard lightly the discipline of the Lord, nor be weary when reproved by him. For the Lord disciplines the one he loves, and chastises every son whom he receives.'

7 It is for discipline that you have to endure. God is treating you as sons. For what son is there whom his father does not discipline? 8 If you are left without discipline, in which all have participated, then you are illegitimate children and not sons. 9 Besides this, we have had earthly fathers who disciplined us and we respected them. Shall we not much more be subject to the Father of spirits and live? 10 For they disciplined us for a short time as it seemed best to them, but he disciplines us for our good, that we may share his holiness. 11 For the moment all discipline seems painful rather than pleasant, but later it yields the peaceful fruit of righteousness to those who have been trained by it.

12 Therefore lift your drooping hands and strengthen your weak knees, 13 and make straight paths for your feet, so that what is lame may not be put out of joint but rather be healed (Heb. 12:1–13).

View your present afflictions in this light, as
chastisements of love; and then let your
own heart say whether love
does not demand praise.

PHILIP DODDRIDGE

OUTLINE

*D*rawing together all the strands we have considered, what conclusion do we arrive at? If the all-wise, sovereign God, who is working out all things for the good of his people, sees fit to make use of suffering in his children's lives, how are we to react to such suffering? The world around us views suffering with horror, and reacts in a variety of ways. Some seek to deny the reality of suffering and refuse to accept it. Many spend their whole lives in a relentless drive to avoid it altogether. When it does strike (as inevitably it will), these same people often manifest either anger, self-pity or stoical resignation. How does the Christian response to suffering differ from these?

There are at least four major elements in the armoury of the believer facing affliction.

Firstly, the Christian casts himself on God, taking immediate refuge in the one who is sovereign over the affliction, and who has the authority to remove it (*Psa.* 18:1–6).

Secondly, knowing that God's sovereignty is above any satanic instrumentality, he responds to the affliction as a possible 'wake-up call' from heaven, for the purpose of dealing with unresolved sin (*Psa.* 119:67).

Then thirdly, if after repentance and prayer the difficulty remains, the believer bows to the infinite wisdom of God and rests in the assurance that the Lord has a loving, just, and wise purpose in bringing this 'thorn in the flesh' into his life (*Job* 23:10).

And finally, remembering that his suffering is spiritually productive for him (*Rom.* 5:3–4) and for others (2 *Cor.* 1:6), as well as keeping in view the vastly superior glory that awaits him, he rejoices (*Rom.* 12:12).

QUESTIONS

1. If according to Hebrews 12:1–3, Jesus is our great model and example, what clues does his experience give us as to the likelihood or otherwise of

suffering? What, on the other hand, was the ultimate outcome of his endurance (and will be of ours too – see 2 *Tim.* 2:12a)?

2. In what light does Hebrews 12:5–11 invite us to approach our sufferings? Are you doing this? What is God's over-riding fatherly motive in this painful 'education programme', and what is he aiming to produce by it?

3. What reasons do Christians have to rejoice in their sufferings, rather than merely to 'grin and bear' them? (see *Rom.* 5:3–4; *Col.* 1:24; 2 *Cor.* 4: 16–18).

Some Other
Banner of Truth Titles

All Things for Good

THOMAS WATSON

'To know that nothing hurts the godly is a matter of comfort; but to be assured that ALL things which fall out shall cooperate for their good, that their crosses shall be turned into blessings, that showers of affliction water the withering root of their grace and make it flourish more; this may fill their hearts with joy till they run over.'

This was the hope of the seventeenth-century Puritan Thomas Watson in publishing his exposition of Romans 8:28: 'All things work together for good to them that love God, to them who are the called according to his purpose.' He gives the biblical answer to the frequently-asked question, 'Why do bad things so often happen to good people?'

'A classic of Puritan devotional writing and an excellent introduction to the Puritans.'
EVANGELICAL TIMES

'A delightful book . . . highly instructive.'
CHRISTIAN LITERATURE WORLD

ISBN 0 85151 478 2
128 pp., paperback

Conflict and Triumph:
The Argument of the Book of Job Unfolded

WILLIAM H. GREEN

As well as casting a great deal of light on the over-all meaning of the book of Job, this study helps 'the afflicted child of God' to draw 'the waters of consolation from this inspired and copious source'.

'Thoroughly Reformed, warmly pastoral and deeply devotional, this is a book I thoroughly enjoyed . . . I recommend it highly.'

REFORMED THEOLOGICAL JOURNAL

'This is an eminently readable exposition, full of the most helpful practical comments and is excellent value . . . Warmly recommended.'

EVANGELICAL TIMES

Here is a classic Christian study that has withstood the test of time and is now again available for a new generation of readers.

MIDWEST BOOK REVIEWS

ISBN 0 85151 761 7
187 pp., paperback